Great day to you! My name is Queenella Gibson. I am a licensed Realtor in New Jersey and a Real Estate Coach. I believe personal development and becoming a master of your world within is the key to your success.

When I was a little girl, I had a lot to say but no one to talk to. I noticed my mom had the same challenge that I did. My mom had a journal and that was her way of getting her words out.

CoachWithQueen.com

A way my mom felt seen and heard was through writing. She would write letters to God each night before bed and that was her therapy. I followed the same path and decided to share a few letters that I have written.

My mom's daily practices has been an ultimate guide for me. I hope my journey, exposing my strengths and my weaknesses, will be a road map to creating a better inner world for you.

Queenella Gibson

CoachWithQueen.com

TABLE OF CONTENTS

CoachWithQueen.com

5. A POWERFUL WEAPON

While under attack, fight with a smile. Your mind, body and soul will go to war with you. 15

6. BE STILL & BREATHE

Never make a permanent decision off a temporary emotion or ideal. Be still. 17

7. IT'S OK TO SAY "NO"

Your energy is low. Not much left to give. How much will it cost you to say "Yes"? 19

8. THE WELLNESS WORKSHEET

Check in with yourself each morning and night. Know yourself. We change daily. Discover who you are and where you are today. 21

CoachWithQueen.com

This book is dedicated to Sheonna, Malachi, Regina, Aarianna, AuntieSis, Christina, Rosalyn, Julia, Alma, Melissa, AuntieMommy, Taliah, and Mom. My Tribe!

FEELING..

by definition is an emotional state or a reaction. Depending on the conditions of your mind is how you will **feel**.

If you **think** "I'm lonely...no one wants my company" you will **feel** sad. If you **think** "I am loved and cared for" you will **feel** safe. If you **think** "everything is going well...I'm living my best life" you will **feel** happy and confident.

Your **feelings** are a reaction to what your mind **believes**. Your emotional state is the result of the conditions of your mind. Your mind is where it all begins.

If you're like me, an **over-thinker,** one minute you will **feel** great and the next minute you **feel** like a complete failure. Control your **thoughts** and become a master of your **emotions**.

Question: Ever **felt** anxious without having a **thought** and not understand why?

Scientist call those "triggers". Your mind is responding to a situation without you knowing. **Feelings** of fear, sadness, or anything negative may be a result of past traumatic experiences and in this case, how do we control our **thoughts** if we can't identify them?

Can we ever be masters of our **emotions**? Questions I could never answer but here's what I practice...

Queenella's Affirmation: Sit up straight. Relax your shoulders. Take 3 deep and slow breaths. Now say...I can't control a world created outside of me, but I will control my world within. My world is where I am needed most. I am peace, I am joy, I am powerful, I am secure, I am love, and I am loved. No one can break me down.

LET GO

I felt tied to this idea of myself and could not cut loose. Like a rope with strands of bad energy, fear, hate, and doubt all braided together tying me up with my hands behind my back and feet to the chair.

I would cry out for help in hopes that someone would rescue me but I refused help each time someone tried. I could not let anyone in. I never gave anyone the opportunity to get close enough to hurt me.

It wasn't that I didn't trust anyone, I didn't trust Queenella. I struggled with these issues. When you don't trust someone you have a difficult time forming a relationship. Well, I had a difficult time forming a relationship with myself.

CoachWithQueen.com

One day it's "I don't need this" and I would act it out. Then when it's gone, I fight for it back. In the heat of the moment I'll say things and regret them later. I felt I didn't have control over my thoughts, my mouth, and emotions. I wasn't in a space to receive care or love from anyone.

I was so confused and known to break hearts. I would abandon people without warning. Especially when things seem too good to be true. I would end a healthy relationship in fear that it may all be a lie. I felt it was wrong to think this way and because I did, I wasn't worthy of a committment. I wasn't a woman designed for love.

Now as a realtor, you have to always pretend as though everything is just fine. Your phone rings non stop throughout the day.

You don't want to miss any opportunities. So with a face full of tears, you must answer every call. If you're a team leader, coach or a mentor, your mentees are relying on you to bring that positive energy everyday to every meeting.

So, I'd wake up. Dry my eyes. Log into zoom for each call session and smile. Game face on 24/7. No days off. No breaks. This is what my life has been like for the last year and I have had enough.

A situation in my past left a scar. This scar was a mark replacing a part of my heart that was once beautiful. This situation made me weak.

It began to show in my weight loss, me shaving my hair, and an obvious downward turn in my business activity.

It's true when they say the only person that can save you is YOU. If you want to reduce stress and improve productivity, you must find your way back to a position of power.

Don't allow past trauma to affect your choices today. If you don't feel strong enough to break through, cry out for help and allow someone to cut the rope. When they do, don't hold onto that rope. Let go!

Queenella's Affirmation: My fears aren't real. What is real is what I am experiencing right now. I must let go of whatever negative energy I have inside. I am beautiful. Even my scars are beautiful. They tell a story of how strong I am. My past does not define me and will not control my future. I am peace, I am love, I am whole, and I am well.

Don't Overheat

I stay up when I want to sleep. I want to stay home but I must support those I love and care about or they'll be so disappointed in me.

I want to let go of this client who doesn't seem to be serious but after working with her for almost a year now, I'd hate to not be compensated for my time.

Sometimes I over promise. I always strive to be the best to get the job done with everything I do. I want to give everyone an experience. I want to be memorable.

This way of thinking is so unhealthy for me. Why do I care so much?

When a system (you) overheats, it can break down. My passion, motivation, and energy broke down in 2020. If only you knew my story. I had nothing left to give. It was then that I decided not to let the machine that keeps me going overheat and burn out.

I decided to care for myself the same way that I care and make sacrifices for others. I decided to take some time off and de-stress.

Queenella's Affirmation: My worth is not defined by the tasks that I complete. What is meant for me will come and I will be ready for it when it does. It's ok to rest. Resting my mind, body, and spirit when necessary is a task that I must complete. I, too, am a priority.

Your Tribe

"I don't have anyone that I can talk to", "I feel alone", "No one cares", "No one loves me", "I can't do this anymore". Those were the words I'd say, looking in my bathroom mirror right before I decided I couldn't go on another day.

The weight was too heavy for me to carry. Painful thoughts I strongly believed were true. I didn't feel like myself. I didn't breathe the same. I didn't know what else to do.

In 2020, at the age of 33, I experienced a bad breakup. Not just any breakup. It was a breakup that almost cost me my life. It was a unity of 12 years with an individual that was everything to me. Someone I would have done anything to protect and would have done everything for.

It was a cold Sunday morning in January when I learned there was someone else that felt the same as I did about this individual. Not only did she feel the same but was experiencing this individual the same way as I did.

I learned about this woman a day before my son's 14th birthday. This was not the way I wanted to celebrate.

January 26 of 2020, I remember missing my flight to San Diego for an event put together for coaches, their mentees, and realtors. I missed my flight because I could not leave my bedroom. I cried all day. It was also the day a famous basketball player and his child had died in a plane crash. On this day, the world stood still.

It was as though the world was mourning with me. The death of an athlete everyone loved and admired while I mourned the death of who I thought this person was but now no longer exists in my mind.

Who I thought he was and would be for the rest of my life took his last breath that day.

There was great sadness in every corner of my mind. It was then, I truly felt cold, depressed, and completely lost. I had no idea who I was or who I wanted to be. My identity, before my relationship had failed, was a mom and someone's life partner. These two roles I thought had no expiration date.

This is who I am until the day I die..and so I tried.

In the attic, a dark room, I laid there each day in a fetal position crying my heart out. It felt like my head exploded from being attacked by so many thoughts. I was being kicked in the head repeatedly thinking I wasn't good enough, how happy she may be to have him, I could clearly see them laughing and holding hands. I was under attack and I didn't fight back. I just laid there and took every beating.

One evening, I called my cousin crying. I don't remember much of what happened that day. I only remember standing at the top of my stairs and wondering if I took a leap would I die. Death will stop the pain and maybe then he'd realize the damage he has done. My kids were all asleep at the time.

I remember my cousin yelling and saying to me "don't you ever say that again".

It was then that I realized I had lost my mind. "Did I just say that out loud?"

When life is too much for me, I know who to run to. There's a book I have with a list of names of people I can call no matter the time of day or night, they will answer. A list of people I can laugh with, cry on, or just sit with in silence.

Where's your tribe? Who will be there to help rebuild you, nurture you, love on you, and protect you. Who will look for you when you're lost? Who will do everything in their power to save you?

I encourage you to make a list of your tribe today. When you feel attacked, run to your tribe, and talk about your problems.

Never be afraid to ask for help. Asking for help doesn't mean that you are weak. Never allow your negative thinking to win. You are not alone.

This is not the way your story ends. Keep fighting!

Queenella's Affirmation: Love is attracted to me. Peace is attracted to me. My heart is healing. I will get through this. I am grateful for the blessings and lessons I gained in my pain. I will be better. I am better. I am not alone.

A Powerful Weapon

When you've done your best but your client is still unhappy, smile! When your deal falls through at the closing table, smile! After a long day at work and you're returning home to a mess made by your children, smile!

You can brighten any day when you find a reason to smile.

Smile, because no one is perfect. Smile, because although your deal fell through, a lesson was learned that could potentially save you more money and open doors for more opportunities in the future. Smile, because your children are alive and well.

Sadly, not many can say they are parents and some parents can't say their children are still with them today. So, again, smile!

Sometimes you win in life and sometimes you learn. Regardless of what the results are in the end, be happy that you're still alive and able to experience them.

Queenella's Affirmation: My smile is beautiful. My smile is powerful. My smile is a weapon that can protect me from those that hate. I choose today to be happy. I choose today to be grateful. When I fight with a smile, my mind, body and soul will go to war with me.

Be Still & Breathe

Don't say anything. Don't do anything. Just breathe.
Focus on the tip of your nose as you breathe air into
your body. Be still. Don't make any decisions today
that may change tomorrow and forever. Try your
best to turn your stress into calm. It's happening
again, but you've got this.

It always happens to me. I can see an image while
scrolling on social media and there's a trigger. It
quickly shifts my mood. My mind begins to wander
off into darkness and it stays there. I have to pull
myself out. I need to reposition myself. This is
uncomfortable and it's not where I want to be.

I have to release the poison, the pain, the doubts,
the fear, the insecurities, all negative energy that
I've attached my thoughts to.

My mind is telling me to panic when there's nothing to worry about. I know that what I focus on becomes powerful. It starts in my mind and then I make it a reality. So I suffer both in my mind and when it happens, that's if it happens. If it doesn't, then I will still worry because I think someday it will. Torture!

If you desire to be happy, focus on what makes you happy. If you want peace, tell yourself to be peaceful. Don't wait for situations to change, change your situations by believing you can have anything and everything that belongs to you. No one can stop you but YOU!

Queenella's Affirmation: It's not who will let me, but who will stop me. I'm stepping into my desired position without permission because I belong here.

IT'S OK TO SAY "NO"

No! Nope! Not today! I decline. Not interested. Not right now. Absolutely not. I'm unavailable.

Pick one. Instead of having an "off day", just take a day off. Not having balance is hurting you. Working 7 days a week...no me time, family time, or a day to reflect doesn't serve you.

This time is designated for "me". Time to unplug and unwind. Time to relieve any stress and to balance my mood. This is the time that I set aside for myself and I will choose to do whatever makes me happy. If it's baking cookies for my kids, taking a hot bath, reading my favorite book, or doing nothing at all...that's my business.

Say no and don't feel bad. When there's a constant need to say "yes" or to do for others, things will get toxic.

Saying "yes" all the time and having no boundaries can negatively impact you emotionally, physically, and mentally. This could lead to more stress, anxiety, depression, and even burnout.

You are a priority! This is the time where it's ok to be selfish. This is the time where it's ok to say "no".

Queenella's Affirmation: I will say "no" whenever necessary. I am aware of my needs and I choose me. Saying "no" is easy. I control my day and my life. I don't have to do anything I don't want to do.

The Wellness Worksheet

Check in with yourself. Know where and who you are today.

What are three things that I am grateful for?

_____

_____

_____

What am I holding onto and need to let go?

_____

_____

_____

How am I feeling right now? What can I do to care for myself today?

_____

_____

_____

Made in the USA
Middletown, DE
03 November 2023

41193830R10015